David Grant

A PROFILE

Verna Wilkins
illustrations by Nick Spender

Tamarind

DAVID GRANT – BLACK STARS
TAMARIND BOOKS 978 1 8485 3014 1

Published in Great Britain by Tamarind Books,
a division of Random House Children's Books
A Random House Group Company

This edition published 2009

1 3 5 7 9 10 8 6 4 2

Set in Sabon

TAMARIND BOOKS
61–63 Uxbridge Road, London, W5 5SA

www.tamarindbooks.co.uk
www.kidsatrandomhouse.co.uk
www.rbooks.co.uk
Addresses for companies within The Random House Group Limited can be found at:
www.randomhouse.co.uk/offices.htm
THE RANDOM HOUSE GROUP Limited Reg. No. 954009
A CIP catalogue record for this book is available from the British Library.
Printed in China

Contents

CHAPTER ONE
The Trip

THE YEAR IS 1959. The place is Jamaica. A three-year-old boy and his mother are speeding along a rough, winding road. The boy is quiet. His mother is nervous.

"Make haste!" Mother urges the driver from the back seat of the car. "We have a ship to catch."

She is holding two passenger tickets for the boat that will take them to England.

The engine of the old car screams in protest as they hurtle along the road. Worn-out tyres screech around hairpin bends and the driver yells at farmers walking on the road with their lazy cows.

The ride ends at the docks, in Kingston, the capital city, and they scramble out. Lugging heavy cases and pushing through the crowds, they work their way towards the ship.

Mother waves her tickets.

Everyone tries to help, moving out of the way and pushing mother and son forwards.

"Hurry! Hurry! Hurry!"

A voice from nowhere booms. "Sorry madam. You are too late! Stand back everybody!"

The ship's siren bellows its final farewell.

High up on the deck of this massive ocean liner, passengers wave frantically to those standing on the docks below. Tearful relatives turn away.

David and his mother stand by their suitcases as the enormous ship gracefully slips away into the wide open seas without them.

A kind man offers some sympathy. "You miss the boat lady! Never mind. You can catch the next one. They come and go all the time!"

"The fact is," says Mum under her breath, "I never asked for this. Auntie pushed me into this England business! I don't want to leave my home. All my friends live here. I hear from everybody how cold England is. Now they will all think it's my fault we missed the boat."

With a heavy heart, David's mother took his hand and they made their way back to St Andrews, a suburb of Kingston, where they lived.

Three days later, the tragic news reached Jamaica. The ship David and his mother were going to travel on was lashed by heavy storms and sank at sea.

One week later, David and his mother returned to the docks in Kingston, in time to board the *Ascania* to England. They avoided terrible storms in the Atlantic Ocean by sailing the long route around the Cape of Good Hope, the southernmost point of Africa.

CHAPTER TWO
Caribbean People in Britain

THERE HAD BEEN CARIBBEAN PEOPLE living in Britain as early as the 17th century, when Britain conquered the islands to add them to its growing empire. But it was in the 20th century that a greater, mass migration began.

The reason for the migration from the Caribbean to Britain was simple. The people were invited.

From 1939 to 1945, Britain was at war with Germany. Young Caribbean men and women, as well as Asians and Africans from all over the empire answered the call to war. They fought hard and died for Britain and the empire.

When the war ended, the bomb damage was tremendous. Over 300,000 British people had died. This caused a severe shortage of people of working age. The government needed to find more workers quickly.

Some Caribbean soldiers had stayed in Britain after the war and found work. As the country was in desperate need of workers, the government began to actively encourage immigration. Adverts were published in the Caribbean islands, urging people to travel to Britain for work.

St Pancras Station, London,
damaged by bombs, 1942

In parliament and the newspapers there were discussions about bringing people over from all around the Commonwealth. So crafty ship captains, sailing through the Caribbean on their way back to Britain and looking to make quick profits, began offering cheap tickets. Tales of work and riches helped encourage people to make the journey.

One of the first groups of Caribbean people to arrive, came on the *SS Windrush* in 1948. About 500 people were on the ship. Most of them intended to stay only a short time. They wanted to work in the country they had learned to think of as 'the Mother Country' and then return home.

After the *Windrush*, more ships came bringing Caribbean people. Among these were some of David's relatives.

Advert for cheap travel to Britain from the Jamaican newspaper, *Daily Gleaner*, 15 February 1959

Caribbean people worked to rebuild the bomb-damaged cities. They worked in the factories, on the railways and on the London Underground. The National Health Service was set up in 1948 and many immigrants found work in hospitals as doctors and nurses, cleaners and cooks.

They all helped to rebuild a healthy, wealthy Britain.

CHAPTER THREE

Arrival in the UK

ON 6TH JANUARY, 1960, after six weeks at sea, the *Ascania* finally arrived in Southampton. It was dull, dark, deep midwinter.

David stepped off the ship, looked up at the grey skies and whispered, "I don't like it here Mummy! Can we go back home now, please?"

His mother shivered in her light, flimsy coat. She tried to smile through frozen lips to greet the relatives who came to meet them.

David and his mother moved into one room in a large Victorian house at 33 St Marks Rise, Hackney in East London, with David's grandmother.

Their small cooker stood on the landing, just outside the room. The bathroom and toilet were one floor down. The house had three floors. Other members of David's family occupied various rooms.

As soon as David's mother settled in and made the room warm and comfortable, she found a job.

Baby-sitting was not a problem. Members of the family took turns to look after David while his mother went out to work. Soon, however, all the adults were out working, so an English family, the Bomfords, who went to the same church, offered to look after David.

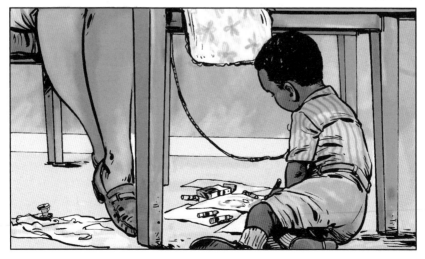

Auntie Marge Bomford was a seamstress and she worked from home. David spent hours under her sewing table with his favourite toys, paper and crayons.

He felt safe in his hideout. He could see Aunt Marge's feet, and could listen to her radio. She never switched it off.

"I wonder…" David now thinks out loud. "Is that where I developed an ear for music? Who knows?"

David aged 7

CHAPTER FOUR

School Days

DAVID'S FIRST SCHOOL was Shacklewell Lane Primary School in Hackney. He was happy there.

School meals were fine for him, because when Auntie Marge looked after him, he learned to like English food. However, some of the children who had recently arrived from the Caribbean found it quite difficult to get used to school dinners.

The memory of a long ago conversation between a dinner lady and a new boy, still brings a smile to David's lips today.

The boy asked, "What's this pap on the plate, Miss?"

"Mash," replied the dinner lady.

"Mash what?"

"Mash potato!"

"I have teeth! I don't need mash up food!"

David enjoyed school and loved reading. By the age of seven, he had a reading age of fourteen, but the books he read didn't in any way reflect his own life and experience.

"I just thought that it was normal to read about two well-off, white kids called Janet and John, their perfect mum and dad, their dog called Rover. Or was it the car that was a Rover? Their lives in middle-class England were a long way from my life in Hackney. Not only for me, as a black child, but for all working-class kids!"

Then, in 1964, when David was seven years old, Muhammad Ali became World Champion in the boxing ring. He made a big impression on David.

"He was the first really confident black man I had seen, and the world was paying a great deal of attention to him. The black people in my life, so far, were humble. They played supporting roles in the world. Here was a leading man, a man who stood tall and said, 'I am the greatest!' And he was!"

Muhammad Ali wearing belt of
World Heavyweight Boxing Champion, 1964

Muhammad Ali was David's first role model. He began to consider what he could be in the future and dared to hope for success.

David's progress through school was uneventful. He did just enough to get by and to keep his teachers and his mother from nagging.

His best subjects were English and History.

"When I was about eight years old, I learned loads of stuff parrot-fashion!" he remembers. "I bored my mother, grandmother and any visiting relatives and friends by repeating the names of all the Kings and Queens of England, from William the Conqueror in 1066 to Elizabeth II, over and over again."

With his sixpence weekly pocket money, David saved three pence and spent three pence on his comic, *The Beano*. However, all the comics, school books and story books had white heroes.

Luckily for David, his mother was aware that he had very few positive role models for success. She set about collecting anything she could find to provide him with images of successful black people to look up to.

"My mother was a major force in my development. At that time, the West Indies Cricket Team seemed indestructible. They were heroes in the cricket world.

"My mother was a firm believer in the old saying that a single picture is worth a thousand words. She collected posters of the cricket team and stuck them up on the walls of our tiny room.

"I learned about the brilliant achievements of the Caribbean cricketers, Conrad Hunte, Wes Hall, Basil Butcher, Lance Gibbs and the heroic Garfield Sobers, the greatest cricketer in the world."

West Indies Cricket Team, 1963
Lancelot Gibbs, back, 8th from left;
Basil Butcher, back row, 9th;
Conrad Hunte, centre row, 3rd from left;
Wesley Hall, centre, 5th; Garfield Sobers, centre, 6th

CHAPTER FIVE

Mother

DAVID REMEMBERS how he became interested in show business.

"My mother introduced me to the magical experience of theatre. While many children never travelled outside Hackney, my mother took me to the Dominion Theatre in Central London to see the *The Sound of Music*, live on stage. It was amazing. Unforgettable.

"Some Saturday mornings I went to the cinema. It was there that my fantasies about being an actor took shape. I never dreamed then, that later in my life, I would have the chance to do a season at the Old Vic (Bristol). In 1997 I was in *Amen Corner* by the great African-American playwright James Baldwin, playing the part of Brother Boxer.

"That same year I had another great acting opportunity, touring with *5 Guys Called Mo*. Then, the following year, I did a magical season in *Oh What a Lovely War!* with the National Theatre.

"I have also been in a couple of short films on Channel 4 TV and had cameo appearances in series such as *The Bill* and *Brothers and Sisters*.

"My love for acting on stage and television will always be with me, but music is my life.

"My Saturday afternoons in the summer were spent playing football with a scout troupe. Sunday morning was church!"

Most Sundays, David was taken to church in the morning and again in the evening. Some sermons were good but some pastors droned on and on. Only the vibrant hymn singing woke David up. He resented those long hours in church and moaned constantly.

"Why is it that you have tummy aches only on Sunday mornings, son?" asked his mother.

Throughout his childhood David regularly visited Auntie Marge, his old baby-sitter. On one Saturday afternoon visit, David saw a long ladder resting against a wall at the side of her house.

He was halfway up the ladder in seconds. The ladder wobbled, the wall crumbled and David crashed to the ground. The scar is still visible on his chin today.

By Sunday morning his face was a mess and his knee was swollen and very painful.

"Ouch! It hurts. My knee hurts! I can't walk. My face hurts! I can't go to church. Ouch!"

"Nothing's broken. Get dressed. It's a special preacher today!" said his mother. "Let's go!"

David groaned. To his utter embarrassment, and the great amusement of the people along the road, his mother and grandmother linked arms and made him hop along between them all the way to and from church. His head hung low and he never looked up once during the grossly embarrassing journey.

That, and so many boring sermons, put him off church for many years. Later in his life, however, David returned to his Christian faith and it's very much a part of his life today.

Chapter Six

A Love of Music

DAVID HAD A GREAT LOVE of music. He loved to sing and had a good singing voice. He listened to music on radio and television.

The Beatles were the popular band while David was growing up. His mother had a photograph of them, with hordes of screaming girls crowding around them.

"I wondered what it would be like singing for a living. But I thought that a career in music was

David aged 9

just a dream. An unachievable dream... When I was growing up, the black singers were American," David recounts. "In England there was Eddie Grant, Errol Brown with his band Hot Chocolate and Bob Marley. Not many others."

Daring to dream, David decided that a career in singing just might work. So, at the age of fourteen, he formed a gospel group called New Life with his cousins. They wrote their own music and performed in youth clubs and bars.

Meanwhile, at school, the time had come to choose a career.

When David was asked what jobs he was considering, he decided on his second choice, which was journalism. He was excellent at English, a brilliant reader and always had good marks for his essay writing.

"I want to be a journalist!" he told the teacher.

The teacher's devastating response was, "You have a snowball's chance in hell of becoming a journalist."

Hope for his second choice of career was dashed. He was never given a reason, but was not encouraged to try to get to university, except by his mother, an amazing woman.

Once, when she was trying to cajole him into further education, David grumbled, "It's easy for you to keep on at me! I have never seen *you* study."

"You will never say that to me again, son!"

His mother promptly enrolled in night school. She took 'O' levels in Science and English and worked as a pharmacy technician for two years. Then she realised that although there were many disabled black people in Tower Hamlets, there were few black social workers available. So she went back to college and did a degree in Social Work. She became the first black social worker for the deaf in her area.

In the Caribbean community, however, some had decided not to struggle against the odds.

David often heard older people say, "Get a job, keep your head down and ask God for help."

David questioned some of the Christian beliefs in his black community. Many people didn't believe in standing up against oppression. But he learned that freedom fighters in Jamaica and other parts of the world, who actively opposed injustice, were Christians.

David believes that, "Fighting for equal rights is not about hating the oppressor, but about loving justice and freedom, and hating what is wrong."

CHAPTER SEVEN

The World of Work

DAVID LEFT SCHOOL at 18 with 'A' levels in English and History.

His first job was in Tandy, an electrical shop. Although David found shop work boring and badly paid, he stayed in that job for a year and a half.

Then a great opportunity came his way. Opposite Tandy, a small shop became empty. David convinced his cousin Joe to join him in a business venture.

They were both keen to get into the world of music, so they borrowed money from family and friends and rented the shop. The young men imported soul records from America and sold them in the UK.

Their first success came when they imported *Songs in the Key of Life* by Stevie Wonder. They had found out that the album would not be released in the UK for three weeks. They quickly bought in a shipment ahead of the release date and sold out in no time. The profit was good.

David continued working in the shop but he was bored and needed to find work which was creative and not just about selling other people's music.

He was still living in Hackney but he no longer wanted to live in a place where wire mesh surrounded the few scraggly trees dotted around the parks and pavements. He loved the countryside and often drove to Epping Forest to watch the sun rise through the trees.

David was a fan of historical television series. At that time, the popular drama *Roots* was being serialised on television.

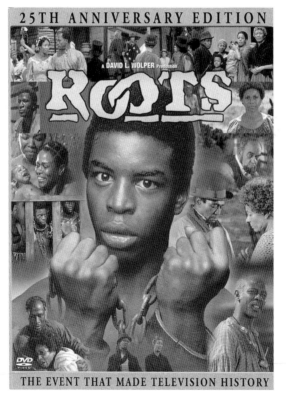

The story line was about the transatlantic slave trade and traced the family history of a young boy from The Gambia in Africa. He was sold into slavery and taken to America to work on a plantation. His descendants handed down his story and the plot followed them through to modern times.

David followed the series. After one painful episode, when the brutality of the plantation owners towards the enslaved people was at its worst, David stayed awake all night. Just before sunrise, he set off for a drive to Epping Forest.

That day, his life changed dramatically.

CHAPTER EIGHT

A New Beginning

IN THE BLEAK, MISTY MORNING, David's car crashed into a lamp post. The horrendous impact blasted him out of the car and onto the road. He was told later on that the steering wheel was rammed backwards into the car and embedded itself deep into the front seat. If he had not been thrown clear, he would have been decapitated.

His only memory of the accident was crawling along the road back to the car. He had lost his glasses and he was cold.

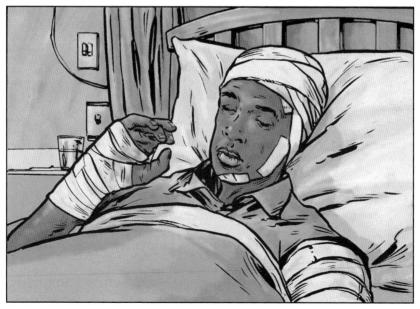

The turning point in his life came as he lay in his hospital bed.

He asked himself, "If that had been the last day of my life, would I have lived the life I wanted to live?"

The response was an emphatic "No!"

He was only 20 years old.

He did not go back to the shop. He handed it all over to his cousin, but worked with him whenever he had free time. He decided to return to his dream of becoming a journalist.

David applied to about fifty newspapers, asking to be taken on as a trainee journalist. He received fifty rejections.

Then one day, listening to Dave Lee Travis on BBC Radio 1, DLT announced that Muhammad Ali, two-times* World Heavyweight Boxing Champion (1964, 1974) had come over from America, and was live on Radio 1 that morning.

---

* Muhammad Ali (originally called Cassius Clay) won the World Heavyweight Boxing Championship again in 1978. But at this point in David's life – it was 1977 – he had only won it twice.

CHAPTER NINE

Meeting Muhammad Ali

DAVID SPRANG INTO ACTION. He phoned his cousin, Paul. "Get your camera. There's something we really have to do. Get here as quick as you can!"

Paul was a brilliant amateur photographer.

The two young men dashed to BBC Broadcasting House in West London and waited at the entrance where a crowd was gathering. At last, a motorcade with the famous Mohammed Ali arrived.

David and Paul sneaked into the group of minders and quickly worked their way to the front. There were quite a few black people accompanying Ali, so David and Paul mingled in and sauntered along with them. They slipped through security right into the BBC studio.

David and Paul sat quietly through the interview and as Mohammed Ali made his way out of the studio, David called, "Mr Ali! Mr Ali!"

The boxer spun around and said, "I wondered when you were going to talk to me. You sneaked in, didn't you? You are not with them," he said pointing to the journalists. "And you are definitely not with us!"

"Can I have five minutes for an interview?" David begged. "Please?"

"No."

"Please? I need a break!"

"Why should I give you a break?"

"Because I'm here. Please Mr Ali!"

"This is the deal. Tomorrow morning, very early, I will go for a run in the park. Come to the Park Lane Hilton Hotel. I might talk to you. I might not!"

By 5.30am the next morning, David and Paul were already sitting in the foyer of the hotel. Ali came down at 8.30.

"I have worked with some of the biggest stars in the world!" David reports. "But I have never seen people stopping their cars in the street to stare, to call greetings and to salute a pedestrian. A very special, world-famous pedestrian.

"As we jogged alongside the great man, a double decker bus stopped. The driver and most of the passengers jumped out. Ali was completely surrounded by dozens of admirers. And there I was standing right next to him! I was elated!

"I scribbled every word he uttered. I was the only journalist present! Eventually, we shook off the crowd and moved on.

"Muhammad Ali turned to me and said, 'You want a photo?'

"'Oh yes... Please. Thanks. Great!'

"The next minute I was shadow boxing with one of the most famous people of the time and Paul's camera was click, click, clicking wildly... David and Goliath in a London street!"

David presented his story to the Walthamstow Gazette and was given a job. He was delighted. That newspaper was part of the Essex and East London Guardian Group, a large local newspaper group. David worked for the paper for ten months.

He had a clean record with his bosses until, one day, he was asked to attend and report on a local council meeting. Instead of following orders, David decided to attend a music event to report on it for a magazine that he worked for on the side.

It turned out that the council meeting was a very important one. The council telephoned the paper to find out why no one had turned up to cover it. David was sacked on the spot.

He then went to work for Island Records to find out how the music industry worked from the inside. This was to be useful preparation for his later work.

CHAPTER TEN

Aiming for Success

DAVID ATTRIBUTES much of his success to the women he grew up with.

His grandmother, his mother and their friends spent time chatting together on many winter evenings.

"They took no notice of a little boy eavesdropping," he remembers. "I learned that what older people regretted were the things they had *not* done in their younger days. They didn't regret the things that they had done."

He learned that they regretted the missed opportunities of their earlier lives!

He learned that despite the careers advice he had been given and the warnings of the people around him, he should pursue his dream. He wanted to be a singer.

He sang his heart out at many auditions but was unable to get work. Eventually, he founded his own soul-funk band, Linx. David was the singer.

After endless days and nights working on their songs, Linx had their first hit in September 1980. But their success was short-lived and some members left.

David and Sketch with the silver disc for 'Intuition'

David and the bass player, Sketch (Peter Martin) continued together and saw six songs enter the UK Singles Charts. 'Intuition' was their greatest success. However, at the end of 1982 they agreed to split.

David then decided to go it alone. He had his first solo hit in 1983 with the song 'Stop and Go' and then had three more hits that year. 1983 was indeed a good year! He was even nominated for a BRIT Award (called BPI Award in those days).

Then, in 1985, he had his biggest hit with 'Could it be I'm falling in love', a duet with Jaki Graham. The song reached number five in the UK Singles Charts

Unfortunately, soon after this, his singing career began to lose direction. He continued to get some work as a backing singer for popular bands, but despite his hard work, success seemed unachievable.

"I really believed that I could do something spectacular!" This strong belief kept him going.

David had read many biographies of famous and successful people. He learned from these true stories that many great people suffered failure but learned to struggle against it in order to finally achieve success.

He learned that success might not come early or all at once! He learned that having achieved success one must work to maintain it. He learned also that during times of failure one must not be disheartened but must continue to work towards success.

He learned that life is "not a destination, but a journey" with all its ups and downs along the way.

CHAPTER ELEVEN

Voice Coaching

IN 1986 David met and married Carrie. They have three daughters.

Carrie had been a dancer on *Top of the Pops* and then worked as a children's TV presenter. She was one of the UK's top session singers, working with Diana Ross, Roberta Flack, Rod Stewart, the Lighthouse Family, Fatboy Slim and many others. She was also a member of the group Sweet Dreams and was in the Eurovision Song Contest aged 17.

David continued to work in the music business until, in 1993, there was a great change in fortune. He and Carrie were asked to put together a small choir to back the group Take That, on a song called 'Pray'.

On the day that they were due to shoot *Top of the Pops*, David and Carrie were rehearsing with the choir, before the show. It was a hot day and the windows were open.

Suddenly, there was a knock on the door. One by one, the members of Take That came in. They had heard their song being sung. They were hugely impressed by the beautiful blending of voices.

"That was amazing! How do you get that sound?" they asked.

David and Carrie explained their teaching methods. Their choir backed Take That and 'Pray' went straight to number one in the UK Singles Charts.

The next day, Take That's management called and asked them to coach Take That. Their voice coaching career was launched with their first clients, Take That, the most popular group in the UK at the time.

David on *Comic Relief Does Fame Academy*, 2007

David has worked with Take That (left) and
Welsh soprano Charlotte Church

The voice coaching business grew and among the singers who came to be coached were the Spice Girls, Charlotte Church, LeMar, Will Young, S Club 7 and Atomic Kitten. David and Carrie then became vocal coaches for *Pop Idol* and *Fame Academy*, the popular television programmes viewed by millions every week.

David says, "Sometimes you don't know how much you do know about something until you are required to do it!"

David is now a well-known, well-loved face on children's TV, entertaining another generation through *Carrie and David's Popshop* on CBeebies.

Omari watching his favourite programme,
Carrie and David's Popshop on CBeebies

CHAPTER TWELVE

Inspiring Others

TODAY, 23 years after they first met, David and Carrie both have successful coaching and television careers. They have been judges on *Fame Academy* and the very popular *Comic Relief Does Fame Academy* in 2003, 2005 and 2007. They both appear regularly on television.

Apart from voice coaching, which he still does, David has been an active participant in *The Wright Stuff,* a chat show that discusses interesting topics

Carrie and David Grant at the MOBO Awards 2008,
Wembley Arena, London

of the moment, and *The Daily Politics* show, with Andrew Neil, talking about the news of the day.

David and Carrie's Popshop is produced by BBC Education and aims to help young children learn music. This reflects David's interest in helping young people to find a successful future.

David presenting at the World Skills UK event, Manchester, 2007

For the same reasons, he is involved with vocational training. He believes that young people who have not done very well at school can have rewarding and successful lives. But they must be helped and encouraged to make the right choices.

Despite a hectic schedule, he makes time to support others and is a great motivational speaker. He constantly works to empower others to reach their full potential.

He encourages young people to go into higher education, but he also points out that we live in a society where many successful entrepreneurs, such as Sir Richard Branson, owner of the Virgin Group Ltd, and Sir Alan Sugar, a businessman, now famous for his television show *The Apprentice*, did not go to university.

David's own life shows that it is important that young people should find their passion and pursue it. He is an excellent role model.

"The greatest lesson my mother and grandmother taught me is that what lies behind you and what lies before you are small things compared to what lies within you."

Photo Credits

Title page: © Gus Campbell.

p.6: © Hulton-Deutsch Collection/CORBIS.

St Pancras Station, August 1942.

p.7: © The Gleaner Company Limited, 1959.

p.12: © Bettmann/CORBIS.

Muhammad Ali August 18, 1964, New York, USA, Bettman Standard RM.

p.14: © Press Association Images.

The West Indies Cricket Team, 1963 (from left to right – back row: George Duckworth (scorer and baggage master), Willie Rodriguez, Seymour Nurse, Michael Carew, Charles Griffith, Lester King, Easton McMorris, Lancelott Gibbs, Basil Butcher, Mr William Pye (physiotherapist); centre: Mr Berkeley Gaskin (manager), Rohan Kanhai, Conrad Hunte, Frank Worrell (capt), Wesley Hall, Garfield Sobers, Alf Valentine, and Mr H. Burnett (assistant manager); front: Deryck Murray, Joe Solomon and David Allan.

p.23: © Wolper Pictures. Licensed by: Warner Bros. Entertainment Inc. All Rights Reserved.

Roots (1977).

p.36: © BBC Photo Library.

David Grant, a vocal coach on *Comic Relief Does Fame Academy*, which started on BBC One on 3 March 2007.

p.37: 517615t – © Ilpo Musto / Rex Features.

Robbie Williams, Howard Donald, Mark Owen, Jason Orange and Garry Barlow - Take That - 1993;

831486b – © NBCUPhotobank / Rex Features.

'The Tonight Show With Jay Leno' TV Series – 2000

– Charlotte Chuch – Air Date 12/30/2000 – Episode 1931
– Pictured: Musical guest Charlotte Church performs
p.39: © Jo Hale/Getty Images.
Carrie and David Grant present an award on stage at the
MOBO Awards 2008, held at Wembley Arena on October
15, 2008 in London, England.
p.40: © Gus Campbell.

Thanks to David Grant and Brian Freshwater for use of their
personal photos.

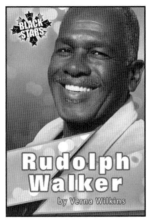
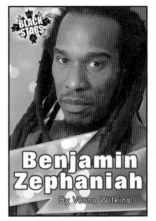
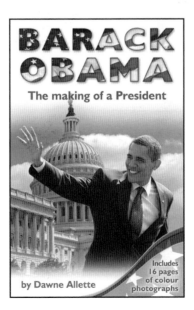